My Christmas Songbook
Music for the Beginning Pianist

with Coloring Pages!

Bergerac

Illustrated by Teresa Goodridge
and Marty Noble

DOVER PUBLICATIONS, INC.
Mineola, New York

All songs available as downloadable MP3s!

Go to: http://www.doverpublications.com/0486780074
to access these files.

Bibliographical Note

This Dover edition, first published in 2017, is a revised edition of *A First Book of Christmas Songs for the Beginning Pianist with Downloadable MP3s,* illustrated by Marty Noble and first published by Dover Publications in 2014. Sixteen new, ready-to-color illustrations by Teresa Goodridge are included in this edition, and begin on page 41.

International Standard Book Number
ISBN-13: 978-0-486-81916-7
ISBN-10: 0-486-81916-7

Manufactured in the United States by LSC Communications
81916701   2017
www.doverpublications.com

Contents

The Pieces Arranged
in Their Approximate Order of Difficulty
(from easy to beginning-intermediate)

This one is for Brandon Lewis,
who saw his first Christmas the year this book was written.

"... it is good to be children sometimes, and never better than at Christmas, when its mighty Founder was a child himself."

Charles Dickens, *A Christmas Carol* (1843)

Christmas songs seem to have been around forever. I remember people singing them when I was a little kid. When I was old enough to learn the words and carry a tune, it was great fun to sing along with everybody else, and to pick out the tunes on our piano with one finger. What a special time of year to wait for!

These days the world seems to spin around faster and faster, and life seems to change quicker and quicker. But those lovely, timeless, sweet and joyous Christmas songs hardly ever change.

Bergerac (Winter 1996)

We Wish You a Merry Christmas

Traditional British

1

O, Come All Ye Faithful

(Adeste Fideles)

English words anonymously
translated from the Latin

Music by J. Reading

Moderate and steady

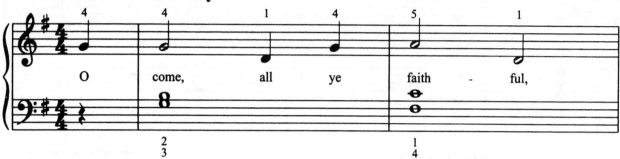

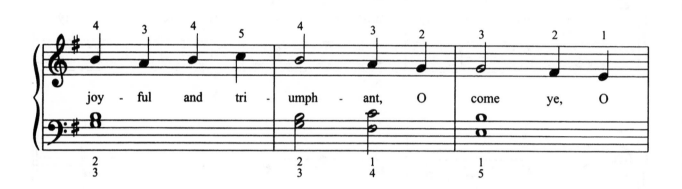

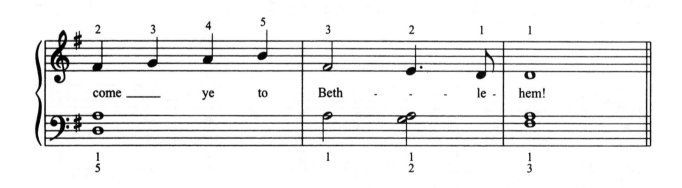

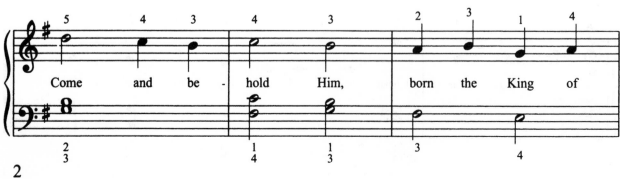

An - gels. O come, let us a - dore Him, O come, let us a - dore Him, O come, let us a - dore Him, ____ Christ ____ the Lord.

Silent Night
(Stille Nacht)

English words anonymously translated
from the German by Joseph Mohr

Music by Franz Gruber (1818)

Tenderly

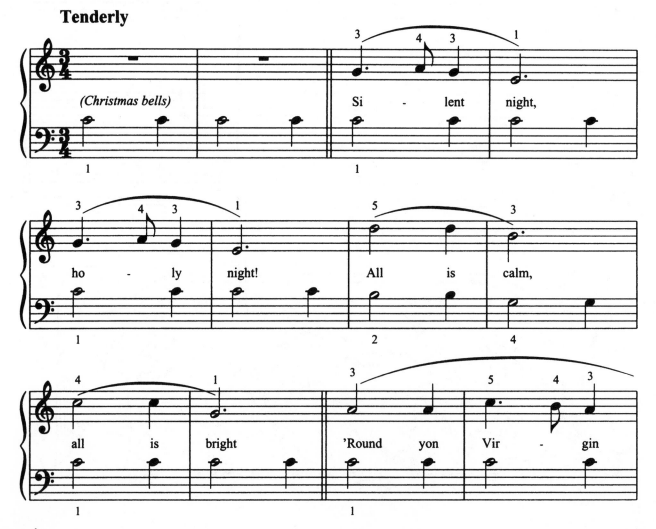

4

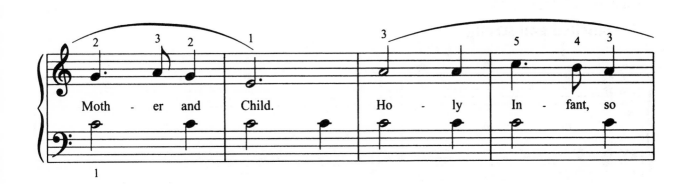

Moth - er and Child. Ho - ly In - fant, so

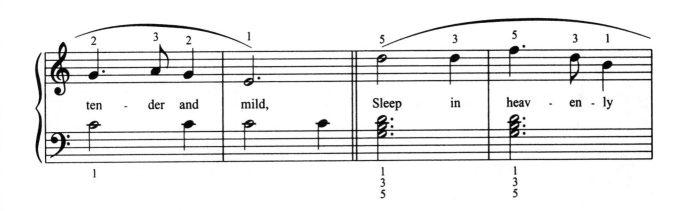

ten - der and mild, Sleep in heav - en - ly

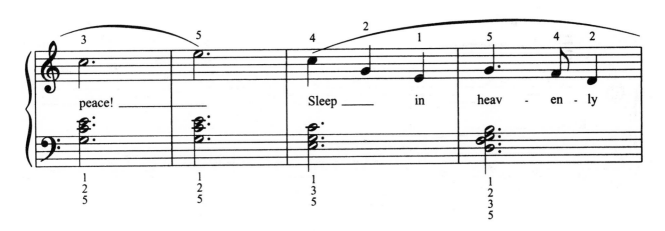

peace! _____ Sleep _____ in heav - en - ly

gradually slower

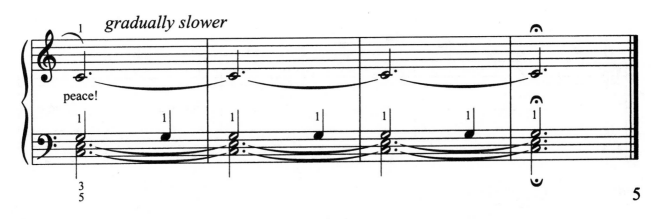

peace!

5

Joy to the World

Words by Isaac Watts (1719)

Composer unknown

Spirited and strong

6

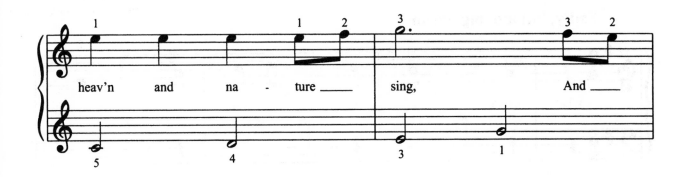

heav'n   and   na - ture _____   sing,   And _____

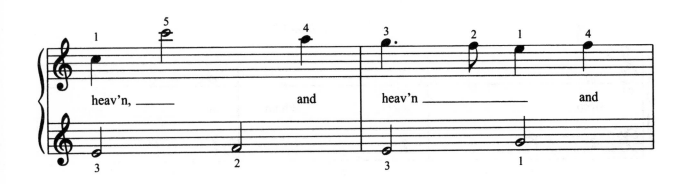

heav'n   and   na - ture _____   sing,   And _____

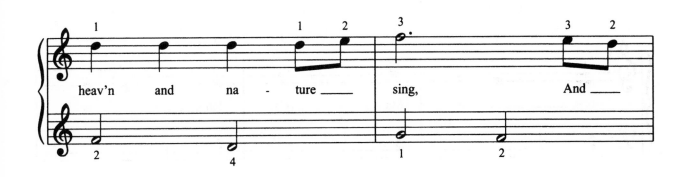

heav'n, _____   and   heav'n _____   and

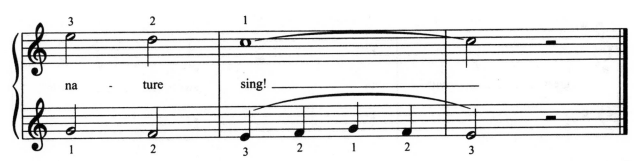

na - ture   sing! _____

What Child Is This?

Words by William C. Dix (19th c.)

Music: "Greensleeves"
(English folk song)

Sadly, but moving ahead

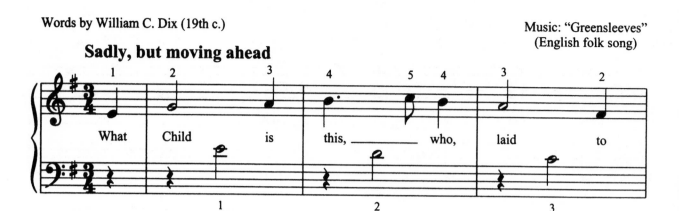

What Child is this, who, laid to

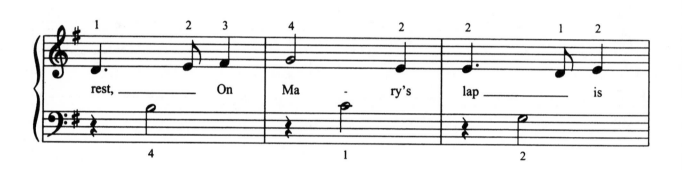

rest, On Ma - ry's lap is

sleep - ing? Whom an - gels

("breath")

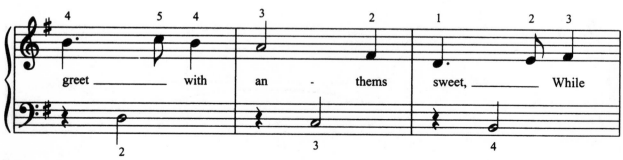

greet with an - thems sweet, While

8

Brighter

gradually slower and quieter

Hark! The Herald Angels Sing

Words by Charles Wesley (18th c.)

Music by Felix Mendelssohn

Bright and sprightly

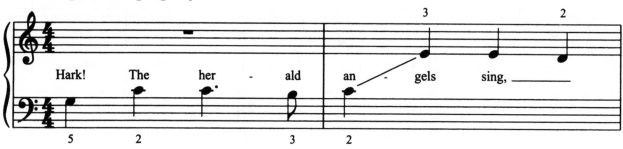

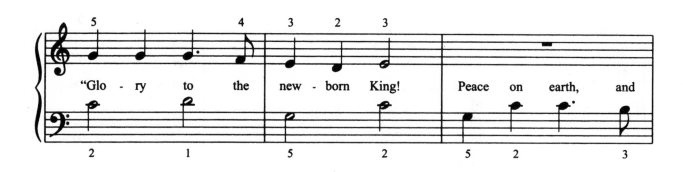

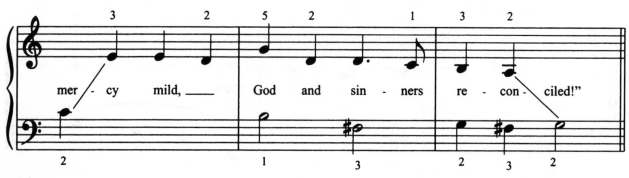

10

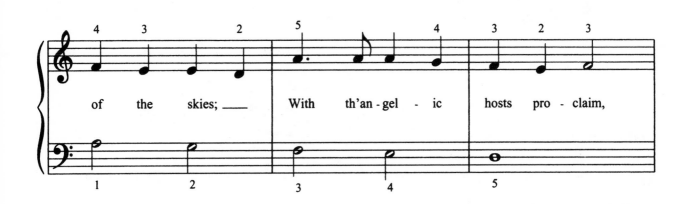

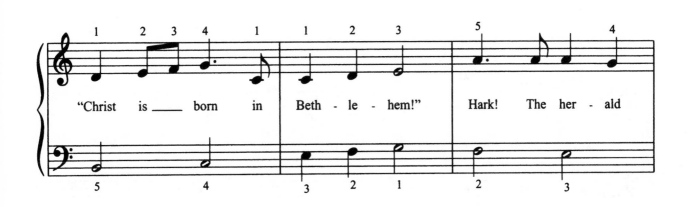

11

The First Nowell

Traditional Christmas song,
possibly French

With good spirit, not too slow

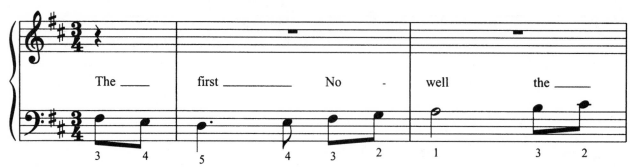

The ___ first ___ No - well the ___

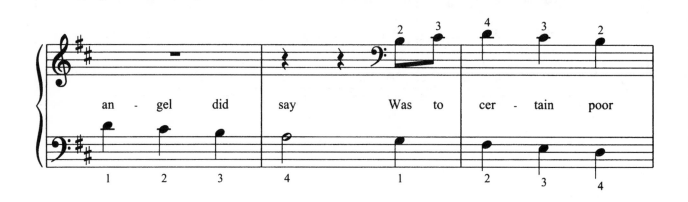

an - gel did say Was to cer - tain poor

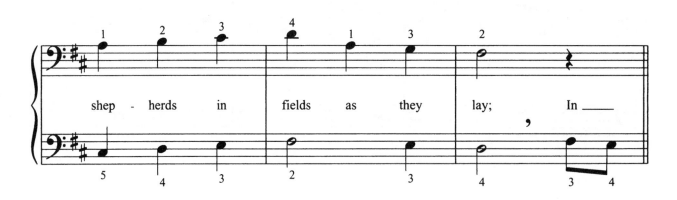

shep - herds in fields as they lay; In ___

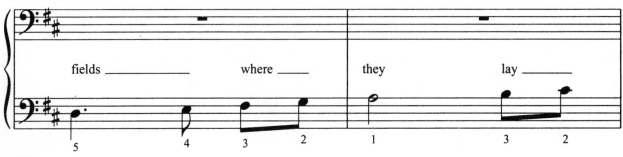

fields ___ where ___ they lay ___

13

O Come, O Come, Emmanuel

English words translated from the Latin
by John Mason Neale (19th c.)

Church chant

Gently flowing

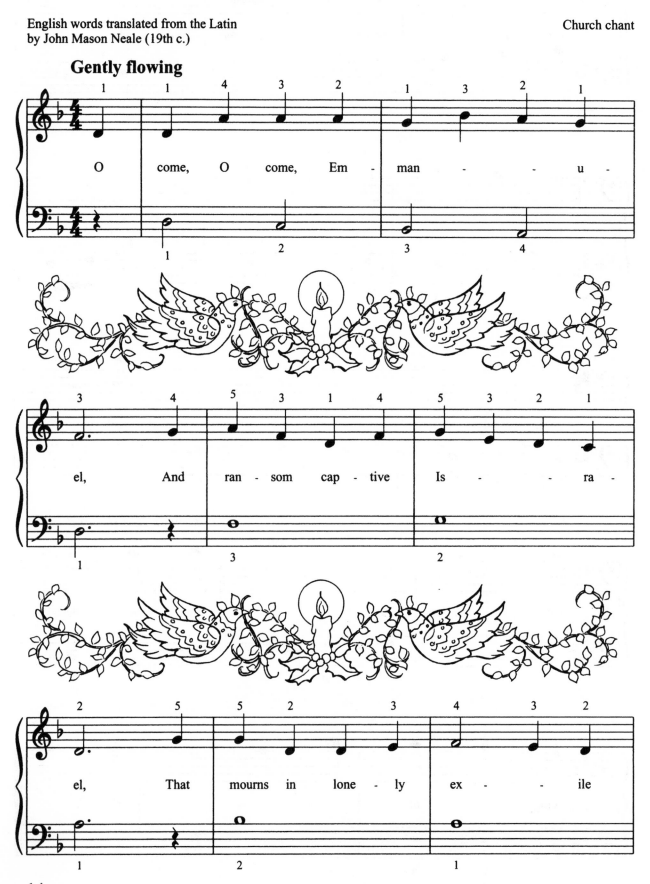

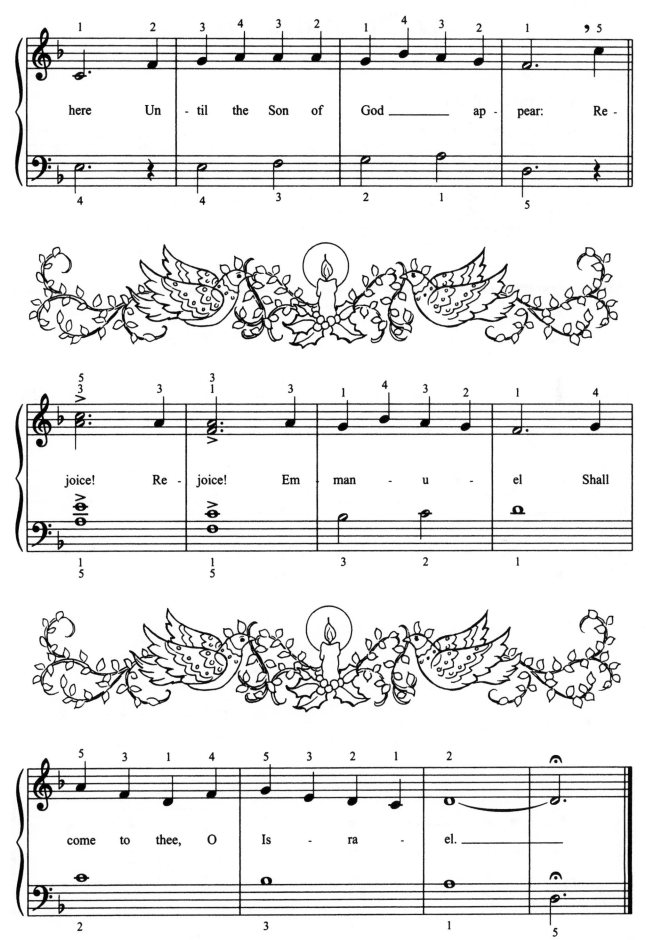

here Un - til the Son of God _____ ap - pear: Re -

joice! Re - joice! Em - man - u - el Shall

come to thee, O Is - ra - el. _____

O Christmas Tree

(O Tannenbaum)

Traditional English words   Traditional German

Very subdued and peaceful

16

Jingle Bells

(One-Horse Open Sleigh)

Words and music by James Pierpont (1859)

Bright, light

Dash - ing through the snow In a one - horse o - pen sleigh, O'er the fields we go Laugh - ing all the way; Bells on Bob - tail ring Mak - ing spir - its bright, What fun it is to ride and sing A

18

sleigh - ing song to - night!

Jin - gle bells,
(Lightly, imitating the jingles on the reindeers' harness)
jin - gle bells!

Jin - gle all the way!

Oh, what fun it is to ride In a

1.
one - horse o - pen sleigh! ___

2.
one - horse o - pen sleigh!

19

Deck the Hall

Words and music by Thomas Oliphant (19th c.)

Quickly, with a lot of spirit

20

Pat-a-pan

Original French words by Bernard de la Monnaye

Traditional Burgundian
dance-song (ca. 1700)

Always moving forward, like a march

[Beat your drum! Sound your fife!
And while you're playing
Ture lurelu pata pat-a-pan
We shall gaily sing about Noël!]

The Coventry Carol

(Lully, lullay)

Words by Robert Croo (1534)   Traditional English

Plaintively, but not too slow

Lul - ly lul - la, thou lit - tle

child, By by lul - ly lul - lay.

O Sis - ters too, How may we

24

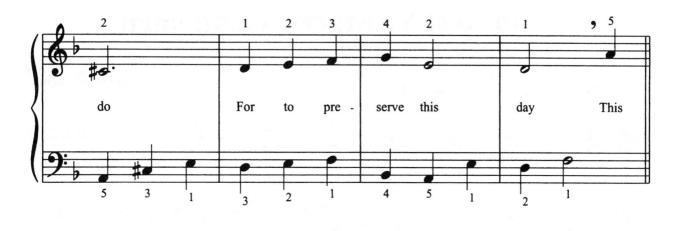

do   For   to   pre - serve this   day   This

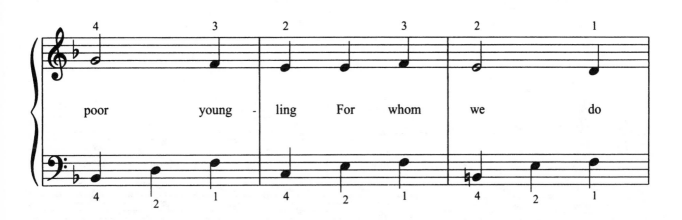

poor   young - ling   For   whom   we   do

sing   By   by   lul - ly   lul -   lay?

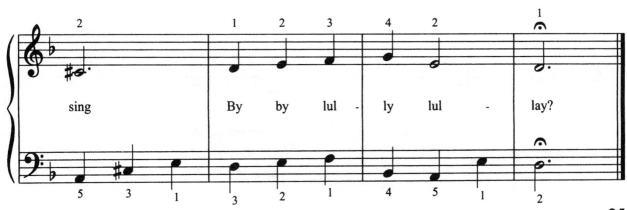

God Rest Ye Merry, Gentlemen

Traditional English

Slow, peaceful, unhurried

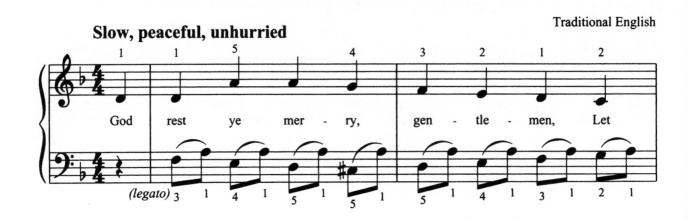

God rest ye mer - ry, gen - tle - men, Let

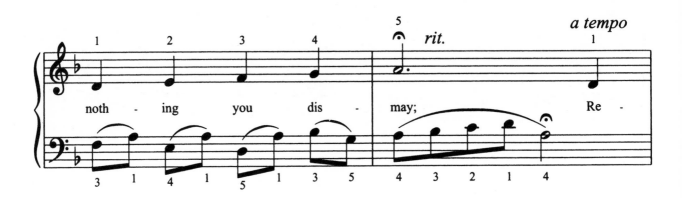

noth - ing you dis - may; Re -

mem - ber Christ, our Sa - viour, Was

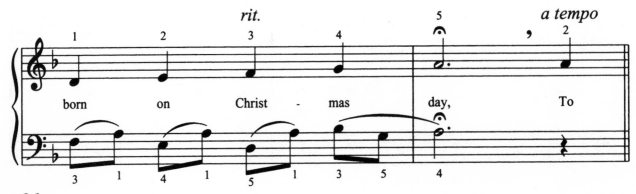

born on Christ - mas day, To

26

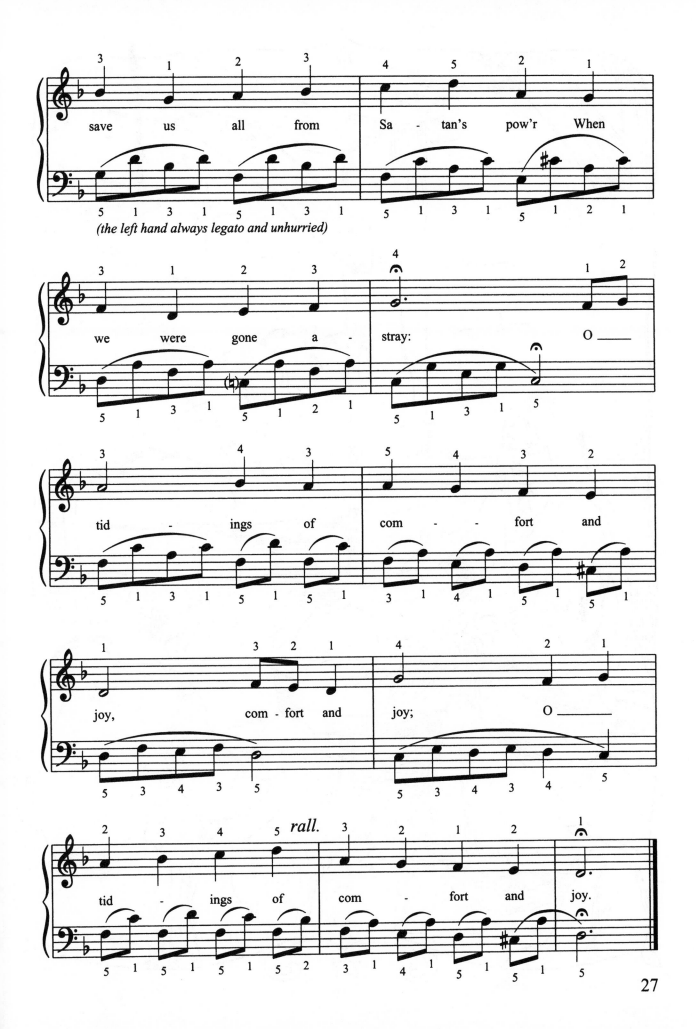

(the left hand always legato and unhurried)

27

Away in a Manger

Anonymous words

Music by James R. Murray ? (ca. 1887)

Gently rocking

The Song of the Birds
(Al veure despuntar)

Traditional Catalan carol

Flowing and expressive

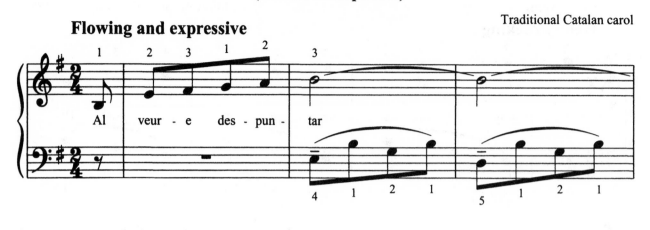

Al veur - e des - pun - tar

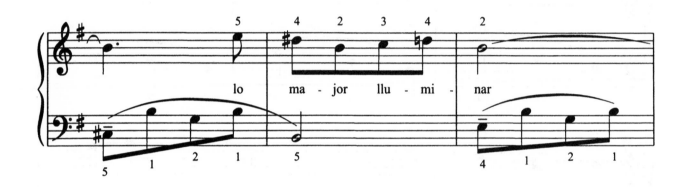

lo ma - jor llu - mi - nar

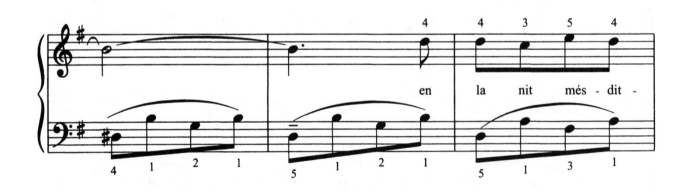

en la nit més - dit -

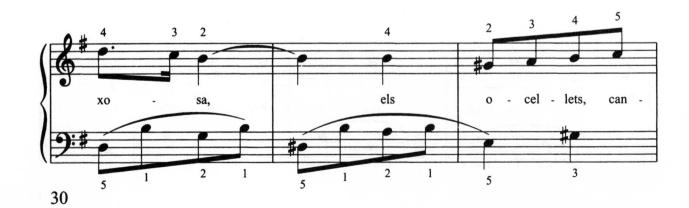

xo - sa, els o - cel - lets, can -

30

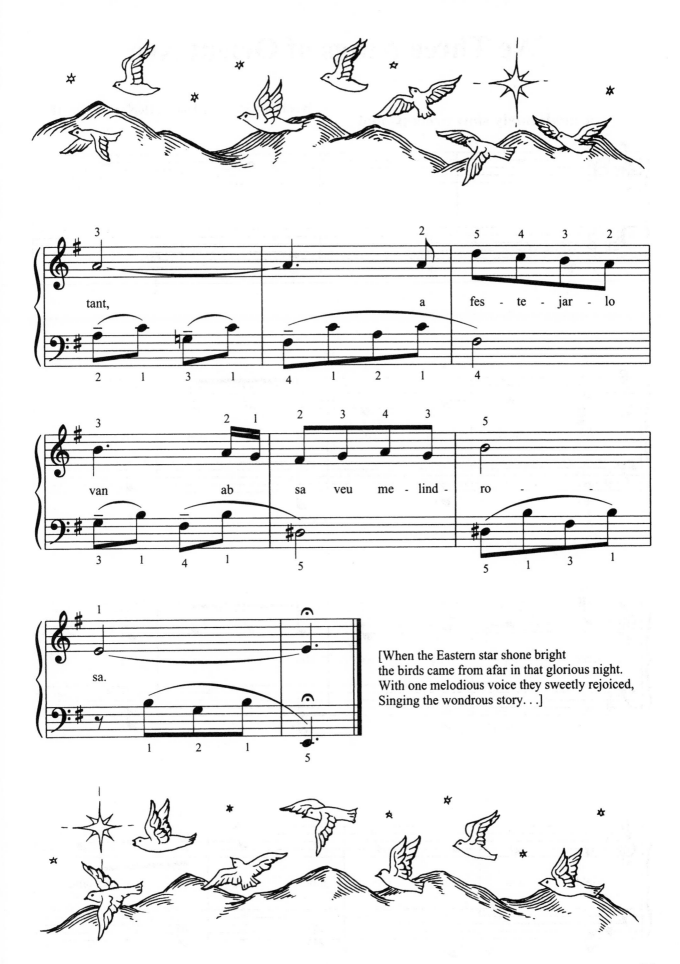

[When the Eastern star shone bright
the birds came from afar in that glorious night.
With one melodious voice they sweetly rejoiced,
Singing the wondrous story...]

We Three Kings of Orient Are

Words and Music by John H. Hopkins, Jr. (ca. 1857)

A moderately slow processional

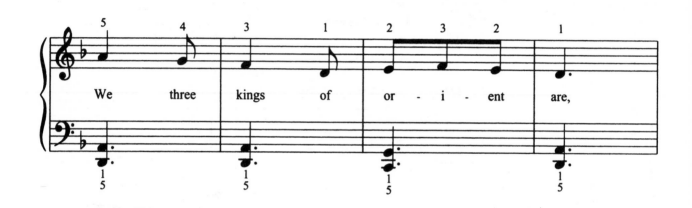

We three kings of or - i - ent are,

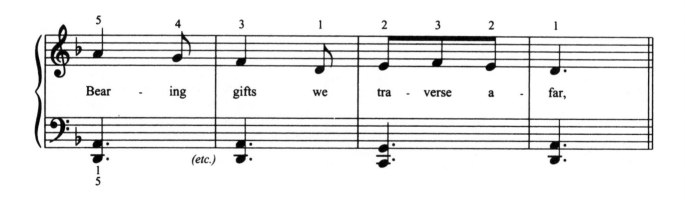

Bear - ing gifts we tra - verse a - far,

(etc.)

Field and foun - tain, moor and moun - tain,

(etc.)

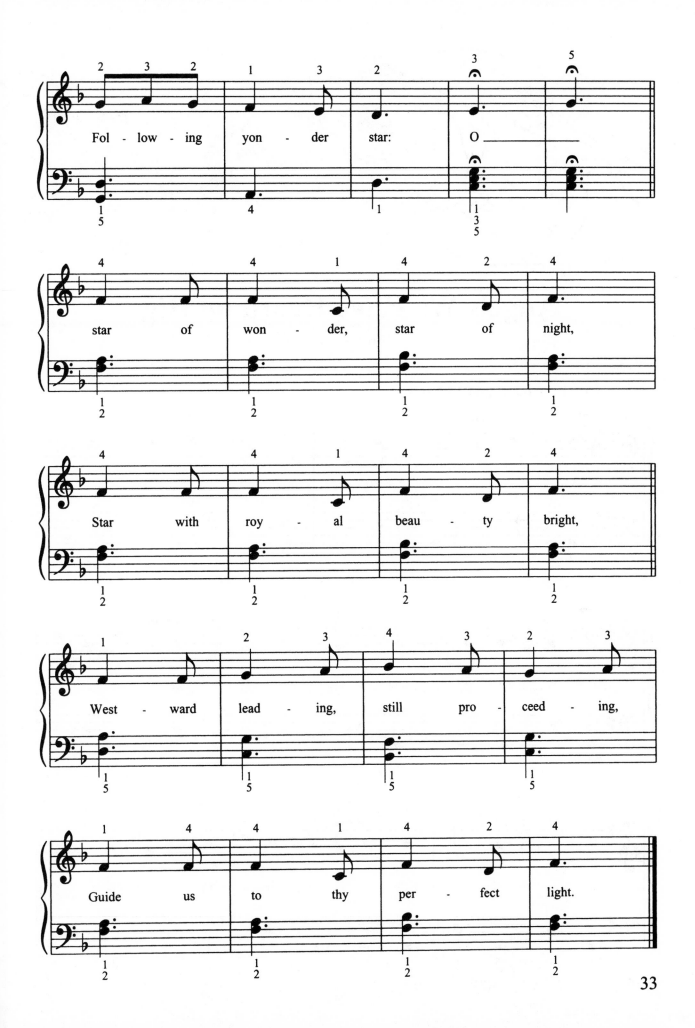

Angels We Have Heard on High

(Cantique de Noël)

Traditional English words

Traditional French carol

Lively, with a good beat

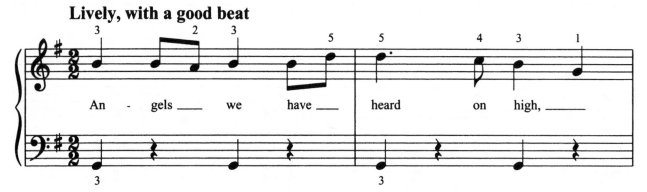

An - gels ___ we have ___ heard on high, ___

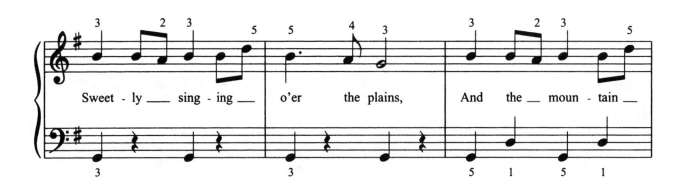

Sweet - ly ___ sing - ing ___ o'er the plains, And the ___ moun - tain ___

in re - ply, ___ Ech - o - ing their ___ joy - ous strains.

Glo - - - - - - - -

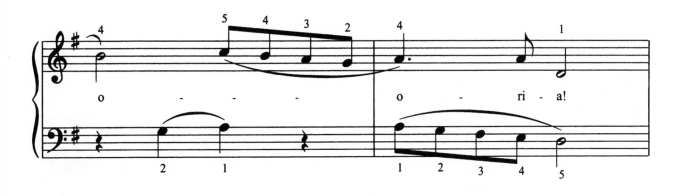

o - - - o - ri - a!

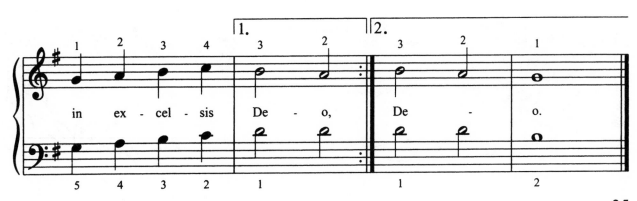

in ex - cel - sis De - o, De - o.

O Little Town of Bethlehem

Words by Phillips Brooks (19th c.)

Music by Lewis H. Redner (19th c.)

Gently, quietly

O lit - tle town of Beth - le - hem, How still we ___ see thee lie! A - bove thy deep and

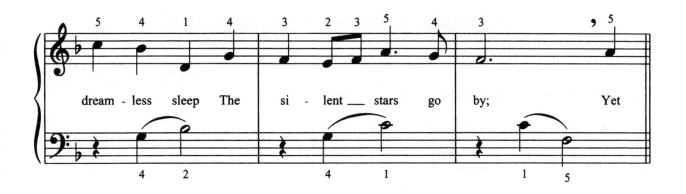

dream - less sleep The si - lent ___ stars go by; Yet

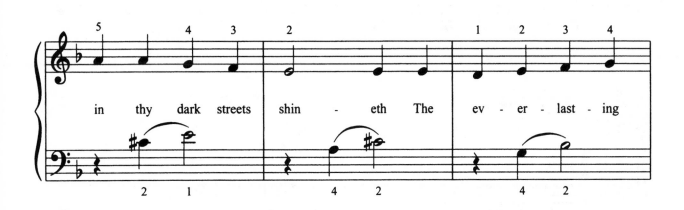

in thy dark streets shin - eth The ev - er - last - ing

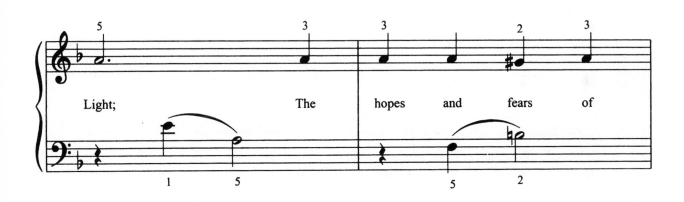

Light; The hopes and fears of

slower 'till the end

all the years Are met in thee to - night.

Shepherds, O Shepherds!

(Pasztorek, Pasztorek!)

Start slowly, then faster at each repetition

Traditional Hungarian dance-song

[Shepherds, O shepherds!
Come rejoice this night
of wonder and joy!]

Repeat as often as you like,
each time faster than before.

We Three Kings of Orient Are